THE LIFE'S SYMPHONY

AYUSHI JAIN

Made with ♥ on the Notion Press Platform
www.notionpress.com

Contents

Contents

Foreword

Life can be a rollercoaster of emotions, full of ups and downs that often leave us feeling overwhelmed and uncertain. But through it all, we must keep moving forward, embracing the journey and all its twists and turns. In this book, I share my own journey, exploring the depths of emotions.

Writing this book was a cathartic experience for me, as it allowed me to process my emotions and make sense of the world around me. I hope that by sharing my thoughts and experiences, I can offer comfort and a reminder that we are not alone in our struggles and that there is always hope for a brighter tomorrow.

So let us embark on this journey together, with open hearts and open minds, as we explore the many facets of life and find hope and strength in the midst of life's challenges.

Acknowledgements

But before we begin, I want to acknowledge the secret friend who has had a profound impact on my life and my writing. This person, whose identity I have chosen to keep private, has been a constant source of inspiration and guidance for me.

They have taught me to live life to the fullest, to embrace uncertainty and change, and to find beauty and meaning in even the darkest moments. Through their wisdom and compassion, this person has helped me to navigate some of the most difficult challenges of my life, and to find hope and healing amid pain and stress. Without their support and encouragement, I may never have found the courage to complete this book or to share my voice with others.

So, to my dearest friend, I offer my deepest gratitude and respect. Your influence on my life and my work will never be forgotten. And whoever reading this, I hope that my words will offer you comfort, inspiration, and hope, as we navigate the highs and lows of this beautiful, mysterious, and endlessly fascinating thing we call life.

Contents

1. The Grip Of Uncertainty

The unknown looms, a shadowy veil,
And anxiety grips you like a vice,
The fear of what may come, the unknown trail,
A weight that's heavy, a costly price.
But fear not, my dear, for you are strong,
And uncertainty can't keep you down for long,
With courage in your heart and hope in your soul,
You can conquer fear and take control.
So breathe deep and take that first step,
For even in uncertainty, there's strength,
With every hurdle, you will find you've kept,
A piece of courage, an unbroken length.

As I navigate through the uncertainties and complexities of life, I am constantly searching for meaning and purpose. Yet, as I grow older, the world seems to become increasingly fragmented and chaotic, making it difficult to find a sense of stability or direction. The past is a distant memory, the future an unknown abyss, leaving me trapped in an eternal present, a never-ending cycle of pain and sorrow.

Life is a journey full of twists and turns, and the road ahead can often be shrouded in uncertainty. The feeling of not knowing where you're headed or what the future holds can be paralyzing, leaving us feeling lost and unsure of ourselves.

The grip of uncertainty can be suffocating. The fear of the unknown, the doubts about our abilities, and the nagging questions about our purpose in life can all leave us feeling overwhelmed and defeated. We begin to question our decisions, second-guess our choices, and lose sight of our dreams.

But uncertainty can also be a source of growth and opportunity. It forces us to step outside our comfort zones, to take risks, and to embrace the unknown. It's a chance to discover new passions, explore new possibilities, and forge new paths.

Navigating life's ambiguity requires courage, resilience, and a willingness to embrace the journey. It means learning to let go of our fears and doubts, trusting in ourselves, and having faith that everything will work out in the end. For in the midst of uncertainty, there is always hope.

2. The Fear And The Courage

The dark clouds gather, the storm draws near,
And fear grips you like a steady fear,
But though the storm may rage and roar,
Your courage can help you face it all.
For even in the face of fear,
There's power to be found,
A strength that's deep, a well that's clear,
A courage that will astound.
So don't be afraid to face the storm,
For courage will light your way,
It will help you stay the course, be strong,
And overcome each and every fray.

As I approach my journey, I am filled with a deep sense of fear. I know that my time in this world is fleeting, that soon I will join the ranks of those who have gone before me. And yet, I am filled with uncertainty, unsure of what awaits me beyond the veil.

The unknown is a terrifying thing, a void that can never be fully understood or comprehended. It is a reminder that there are some things in life that we will never know, that no matter how hard we try, we can never fully grasp the complexity and mystery of the universe.

Fear can be paralyzing. It can leave us feeling trapped, helpless, and vulnerable. It can stop us from pursuing our dreams, taking risks, and living life to the fullest.

The terror of fear can be suffocating. It can make us feel like we're stuck in a dark tunnel with no light at the end. It can rob us of our confidence, our courage, and our sense of purpose.

But fear doesn't have to control us. We can learn to face our fears head-on, to embrace the uncertainty, and to find the courage to move forward. It requires a combination of self-reflection, self-compassion, and taking small steps towards our goals.

By learning to reflect on our fears, practicing self-compassion, and taking small steps towards our By learning to reflect on our fears, practicing self-compassion, and taking small steps towards our goals, we can begin to overcome the paralysis of dread. We can learn to let go of our fears, trust in ourselves, and find the courage to pursue our dreams. For in the end, fear doesn't have to hold us back. We are stronger than our fears.

3. The Many Faces Of Love

Love comes in many shapes and sizes,
In every color of the rainbow,
It can be a whisper, a shout, a surprise,
A constant presence, a steady flow.
For love can heal, love can mend,
It can lift you up and help you stand,
It can be a friend, a partner, a blend,
A warmth that spreads throughout the land.
So cherish every moment, every chance,
To give and receive the love that's true,
For in the end, it's love that will advance,
And help you through the good times and the blue.

4. The Ups And Downs Of Life

Life is full of twists and turns,
Of ups and downs and unexpected burns,
It can be a rollercoaster ride,
With highs and lows that can't be denied.
But though the journey may be hard,
And the road may seem long and dark,
There's always a light to guide your path,
And help you through each and every part.
So hold on tight and don't let go,
For life is a journey, ever so,
A winding road that twists and turns,
But with every step, your spirit learns.

Life is full of both good and bad. The world around us is constantly changing, and it can be challenging to navigate the ups and downs.

The Emotions of life can be overwhelming. They can make us feel like we're living in a never-ending cycle of chaos, uncertainty, and crisis. They can leave us feeling hopeless, helpless, and lost.

But navigating the challenges of a changing world requires resilience, adaptability, and a willingness to embrace change. It means learning to focus on what we can control, finding joy in the small moments, and holding onto hope for the future. By learning to focus on the present moment, practicing gratitude, and finding ways to cope with stress, we can navigate the challenges of a changing world. We can learn to find strength in our struggles, to seek out the good amidst the bad, and to hold onto hope for a better tomorrow. For in the end, the Emotions of life don't have to define us. We are capable of resilience and growth.

5. The Windy Veil - Sadness

A burden that can be hard to abate,
A feeling that can be hard to shake,
A shadow that can make your heart ache.
But though the sadness may be hard to bear,
And the weight may seem too much to bear,
There's always hope to be found,
A way to rise above the ground.
For even in the darkest hour,
There's light that shines with a gentle power,
A kindness, a love, a helping hand,
That can lift you up and help you stand.
So hold on tight and don't give in,
For hope will always be a win,
A light that shines, a beacon true,
That will guide you through and see you through.

Despite the sadness and uncertainty that pervades my life, I find solace in the beauty of the world around me. The gentle touch of the wind, the soft glow of the stars, the sweet scent of a flower - these small moments of beauty give me strength to carry on. They remind me that even in the darkest moments, there is still something worth fighting for.

I find beauty in the simple things, the everyday moments that are so easily taken for granted. A smile from a stranger, the warmth of the sun on my skin, the sound of a bird singing in the distance - these are the fragments of joy that sustain me through the trials and tribulations of life.

Sadness can feel like a heavy weight, pressing down on our hearts and souls. It can be difficult to navigate the depths of this emotion, and to find a way out of the darkness.

But it's important to remember that sadness is a normal and natural part of human emotions. It's okay to feel sad, to grieve, and to process our emotions in our own time and way. By allowing ourselves to feel our sadness, finding healthy ways to cope, and seeking support from others, we can begin to lighten the weight of our burden. We can learn to process our emotions, to find healing in our pain, and to rediscover joy in the present moment.

For in the end, the heavy weight of sadness can be lifted by the power of self-compassion, the warmth of human connection, and the resilience of the human spirit. Let us embrace our sadness, process our emotions, and find the strength to keep moving forward.

6. The Hurdle - Anxiety

Anxiety, thou tempest in the night,
Casting fearful shadows in every light.
Draining out courage and sapping will,
Haunting us with a paralyzing chill.
Through day and night it nips and gnaws,
The scars and wounds leave no pause.
Sapping energy with empty lies,
Forever seeking us to paralyze.
It whispers of fear and dread,
An invisible prison will spread.
Eroding peace and joy within,
Pulling us down again and again.
Clinging like a darkening fog,
Anxiety slowly kills our hopes.
It traps us in an endless night,
Making our life a frozen blight.
Anxiety, agonizing foe,
Spreading chaos wherever you go.
Depression and pain your wake will show,
Draining those seeking joy below.

The constant worry, the racing thoughts, and the physical symptoms can all leave us feeling overwhelmed and exhausted. It can make even the simplest of tasks feel like insurmountable challenges.

Anxiety can make us feel like we're drowning in a sea of worries, unable to catch our breath. It can rob us of our joy, our peace, and our sense of well-being.

But anxiety doesn't have to control us. We can learn to overcome its grip and find a sense of calm in the midst of the storm. It requires a combination of self-care, mindfulness, and seeking professional help when necessary.

By learning to take care of ourselves, practicing mindfulness, and reaching out for help, we can begin to lighten the load of anxiety. We can learn to let go of our worries, trust in the journey, and find peace in the midst of the chaos. For in the end, anxiety doesn't have to define us. We are stronger than our worries.

7. The Imagination's Prison

The imagination is a powerful tool,
A gift that can make us feel like a fool.
For in its grip, we're often trapped,
Unable to break free from its grasp.
The illusions it creates can be so real,
That we forget what we know and what we feel.
And though we try to escape its hold,
We find ourselves lost in a world so cold.
The imagination's prison can be a lonely place,
Where we're left to face our own disgrace.
But if we can find the strength to break free,
We'll find a world that's waiting for you and me.

Imagination is a powerful tool, one that can help us escape the pain of reality. It allows us to create new worlds and new possibilities, to dream of a life that is different from the one we currently have. It's a way to cope with the pain and uncertainty of life.

But the reality is that imagination can also be a trap. We may become so lost in our own fantasies that we lose sight of what is truly important. We may become so obsessed with the perfect life that we forget to live in the present moment. The worst part is that imagination can be fleeting. We may find ourselves unable to escape the pain of reality, no matter how hard we try to imagine something different. But even though it's not a guaranteed escape, I know that imagination can provide a much-needed reprieve from the pain of reality.

8. The Flames of Desire

Desire burns within my heart,
A fire that never seems to start.
It lingers there, a constant ache,
A thirst that nothing can slake.
The flames of passion dance and sway,
And yet, I cannot look away.
For in this fire, I see my soul,
And all the things that make me whole.
But even as I bask in the glow,
I cannot help but feel the woe.
For desire, though a beautiful thing,
Can also leave a bitter sting.

The desire burns inside of me like a raging fire, consuming me from the inside out. It's a never-ending hunger that leaves me feeling empty and unsatisfied. Every day, I wake up with the burning desire for something more, something that I can never quite grasp. It's a constant ache, a feeling of longing that never goes away.

The worst part is that the desire never goes away, no matter how much I try to ignore it. It's always there, lurking in the background, reminding me of what I lack. I feel like I'm always searching for something that I can never find, like a rat running endlessly on a wheel. The more I try to fill the void, the emptier I feel.

The burning hunger is a curse, that I carry with me wherever I go. It's a reminder of my own inadequacy, of my own inability to be satisfied with what I have. It's a constant battle to keep the desire in check, to prevent it from consuming me completely. But I fear that one day, the fire will become too much to bear, and I will be consumed by it entirely.

9. The Illusions

Love can be an illusion, a trick of the mind,
A mirage that we hope to find.
We see what we want to see,
And find ourselves lost in the fantasy.
The illusions of love can be so strong,
That we forget what's right and what's wrong.
We cling to a dream that cannot be,
And find ourselves lost in love's endless sea.
But though the illusions may be sweet,
They can also leave us feeling incomplete.
For love is not just a fantasy,
But a journey that requires bravery.

We all have illusions that we create, whether it's about ourselves or the world around us. We may create an idealized version of ourselves, one that we strive to become but can never fully achieve. We may create an idealized version of the world, one that is perfect and without flaws.

But the reality is that these illusions are just that - illusions. They are not real, and they can lead us down a path of disappointment and disillusionment. We may feel like we have failed because we cannot live up to these illusions, or we may feel like the world has let us down because it doesn't match our idealized version of it.

The worst part is that these illusions can be hard to let go of. We may hold onto them tightly, afraid to confront the reality of who we truly are or what the world truly is. But I know that letting go of these illusions is necessary for growth and acceptance.

10. The Confusion of the Heart

The confusion of the heart can be a cruel thing,
A labyrinth of emotions that make us sing
A song of love and pain and fear,
That leaves us feeling lost and unclear.
We think we know what we want and need,
But in reality, our hearts can deceive
And lead us down a path of sorrow,
Where we're left with no hope for tomorrow.
The confusion of the heart can make us blind,
To the truth that's right in front of our minds.
We cling to illusions and false hopes,
And find ourselves unable to cope.
But though the confusion may seem never-ending,
There's always a way to find a new beginning.
We just need to trust in ourselves and in love,
And let our hearts guide us from above.

The heart is a confusing thing, full of contradictions and complexities. It's a never-ending battle between our emotions and our rational minds, a constant struggle to understand what we truly want. It's like being lost in a maze, with no clear path forward.

The worst part is that the confusion of the heart can lead us down the wrong path. We may think that we know what we want, but in reality, our hearts can deceive us. We may find ourselves chasing after something that we think will make us happy, only to realize that it was never what we truly wanted.

The confusion of the heart can also lead us to doubt ourselves and our decisions. We may second-guess ourselves, wondering if we made the right choice. We may feel like we're stuck in limbo, unable to move forward or let go of the past.

But even though the confusion of the heart is painful, I know that it's a necessary part of the journey. It's through this confusion that we learn more about ourselves and what we truly want. It's through the pain that we grow and become stronger.

11. The Temptation of Lust

Lust whispers in my ear,
A siren song that I cannot hear.
It calls to me, a promise of pleasure,
A temptation that I cannot measure.
The seductive pull is hard to resist,
And yet, I know I must persist.
For lust, though it may seem divine,
Can lead us down a dangerous line.
The pleasure it brings is fleeting and vain,
A momentary high that soon wanes.
And in the end, we're left with regret,
And the bitter taste of lust's cold sweat.

Lust is a seductive voice that whispers sweet nothings in my ear, promising pleasure and fulfillment. But it's a cruel trickster, leading me down a path of illusions that I can never quite catch. It's a cycle of wanting and longing, always searching for something that I can never find. The more I chase after it, the more elusive it becomes.

Lust is a never-ending game, a cruel and vicious cycle that leaves me feeling empty and unfulfilled. It's a hollow promise, a mirage that disappears as soon as I get close. The illusions are like chains that bind me, keeping me trapped in a world of my own making. I am a prisoner of my own desires, unable to break free.

The worst part is that I know it's an illusion, but I can't help myself. The promise of pleasure is too alluring, too tempting to resist. But each time I give in, the emptiness inside me grows deeper. I am left feeling lost and alone, with nothing but my own lustful illusions for company.

12. The Bottled Up Inside

Sometimes the weight of life can be too much,
And emotions swirl, untamed, and such,
But though it may be hard to say,
Expressing yourself can help you find
A way to ease the pain and find release,
To let go of what you hold and find peace,
To face your fears and speak your truth,
And find a path to a brighter youth.
For holding in your emotions can be a strain,
A burden that can cause you pain,
It can lead to stress and anxiety,
And rob you of your clarity.
So don't be afraid to let it out,
To cry, to shout, to scream, to pout,
To let your feelings flow and find,
The freedom that comes with an open mind.

Suppressed emotions can be a heavy burden to carry. The weight of unspoken words can leave us feeling isolated, disconnected, and misunderstood.

The weight of suppressed emotions can be suffocating. It can rob us of our ability to connect with others, to express ourselves, and to be vulnerable. It can lead to a cycle of shame, guilt, and self-doubt.

But unpacking the burden of unspoken words can be liberating. It requires a willingness to be vulnerable, to open ourselves up to the possibility of connection, and to trust in ourselves.

By learning to express ourselves, practicing vulnerability, and trusting in the journey, we can begin to unpack the burden of unspoken words. We can learn to connect with others, find our voice, and feel a sense of freedom. For in the end, the weight of suppressed emotions doesn't have to define us. We are stronger than our silence.

13. The Mask of a Smile

I wear a smile upon my face,
A mask to hide the inner place.
It's there to shield the pain and strife,
And keep me going through this life.
But behind this facade, I hide,
A thousand sorrows deep inside.
For though I try to keep them locked away,
They always seem to find a way.
The fake smile that I wear so well,
Is just a cover for the hell.
And though I wish I could break free,
I fear what others might see.

The smile is a mask that I wear, a thin veil that covers the emptiness inside. It's a constant battle to keep up the charade, to pretend that everything is okay when it's not. But the smile is fading, and I fear that one day, it will disappear completely. Every day, I wake up and put on my smile, hoping that it will be enough to get me through the day. But as the hours pass, the smile fades, and I am left alone with my pain. It's a constant struggle to keep up appearances, to pretend that everything is okay when it's not.

The worst part is that no one sees the pain behind the smile. They see only what I want them to see, a happy and contented person with no troubles in the world. But the reality is very different. The pain is always there, a constant reminder of what I lack. And the smile, once a beacon of hope, has become a burden that I carry with me everywhere I go.

I wear a smile upon my face,
A mask to hide the inner place.
It's there to shield the pain and strife,
And keep me going through this life.
But behind this facade, I hide,
A thousand sorrows deep inside.
For though I try to keep them locked away,
They always seem to find a way.
The fake smile that I wear so well,
Is just a cover for the hell.
And though I wish I could break free,
I fear what others might see.

The smile is a mask that I wear, a thin veil that covers the emptiness inside. It's a constant battle to keep up the charade, to pretend that everything is okay when it's not. But the smile is fading, and I fear that one day, it will disappear completely. Every day, I wake up and put on my smile, hoping that it will be enough to get me through the day. But as the hours pass, the smile fades, and I am left alone with my pain. It's a constant struggle to keep up appearances, to pretend that everything is okay when it's not.

The worst part is that no one sees the pain behind the smile. They see only what I want them to see, a happy and contented person with no troubles in the world. But the reality is very different. The pain is always there, a constant reminder of what I lack. And the smile, once a beacon of hope, has become a burden that I carry with me everywhere I go.

I wear a smile upon my face,
A mask to hide the inner place.
It's there to shield the pain and strife,
And keep me going through this life.
But behind this facade, I hide,
A thousand sorrows deep inside.
For though I try to keep them locked away,
They always seem to find a way.
The fake smile that I wear so well,
Is just a cover for the hell.
And though I wish I could break free,
I fear what others might see.

The smile is a mask that I wear, a thin veil that covers the emptiness inside. It's a constant battle to keep up the charade, to pretend that everything is okay when it's not. But the smile is fading, and I fear that one day, it will disappear completely.

Every day, I wake up and put on my smile, hoping that it will be enough to get me through the day. But as the hours pass, the smile fades, and I am left alone with my pain. It's a constant struggle to keep up appearances, to pretend that everything is okay when it's not.

The worst part is that no one sees the pain behind the smile. They see only what I want them to see, a happy and contented person with no troubles in the world. But the reality is very different. The pain is always there, a constant reminder of what I lack. And the smile, once a beacon of hope, has become a burden that I carry with me everywhere I go.

I wear a smile upon my face,
A mask to hide the inner place.
It's there to shield the pain and strife,
And keep me going through this life.
But behind this facade, I hide,
A thousand sorrows deep inside.
For though I try to keep them locked away,
They always seem to find a way.
The fake smile that I wear so well,
Is just a cover for the hell.
And though I wish I could break free,
I fear what others might see.

The smile is a mask that I wear, a thin veil that covers the emptiness inside. It's a constant battle to keep up the charade, to pretend that everything is okay when it's not. But the smile is fading, and I fear that one day, it will disappear completely. Every day, I wake up and put on my smile, hoping that it will be enough to get me through the day. But as the hours pass, the smile fades, and I am left alone with my pain. It's a constant struggle to keep up appearances, to pretend that everything is okay when it's not.

The worst part is that no one sees the pain behind the smile. They see only what I want them to see, a happy and contented person with no troubles in the world. But the reality is very different. The pain is always there, a constant reminder of what I lack. And the smile, once a beacon of hope, has become a burden that I carry with me everywhere I go.

I wear a smile upon my face,
A mask to hide the inner place.
It's there to shield the pain and strife,
And keep me going through this life.
But behind this facade, I hide,
A thousand sorrows deep inside.
For though I try to keep them locked away,
They always seem to find a way.
The fake smile that I wear so well,
Is just a cover for the hell.
And though I wish I could break free,
I fear what others might see.

The smile is a mask that I wear, a thin veil that covers the emptiness inside. It's a constant battle to keep up the charade, to pretend that everything is okay when it's not. But the smile is fading, and I fear that one day, it will disappear completely. Every day, I wake up and put on my smile, hoping that it will be enough to get me through the day. But as the hours pass, the smile fades, and I am left alone with my pain. It's a constant struggle to keep up appearances, to pretend that everything is okay when it's not.

The worst part is that no one sees the pain behind the smile. They see only what I want them to see, a happy and contented person with no troubles in the world. But the reality is very different. The pain is always there, a constant reminder of what I lack. And the smile, once a beacon of hope, has become a burden that I carry with me everywhere I go.

I wear a smile upon my face,
A mask to hide the inner place.
It's there to shield the pain and strife,
And keep me going through this life.
But behind this facade, I hide,
A thousand sorrows deep inside.
For though I try to keep them locked away,
They always seem to find a way.
The fake smile that I wear so well,
Is just a cover for the hell.
And though I wish I could break free,
I fear what others might see.

The smile is a mask that I wear, a thin veil that covers the emptiness inside. It's a constant battle to keep up the charade, to pretend that everything is okay when it's not. But the smile is fading, and I fear that one day, it will disappear completely. Every day, I wake up and put on my smile, hoping that it will be enough to get me through the day. But as the hours pass, the smile fades, and I am left alone with my pain. It's a constant struggle to keep up appearances, to pretend that everything is okay when it's not.

The worst part is that no one sees the pain behind the smile. They see only what I want them to see, a happy and contented person with no troubles in the world. But the reality is very different. The pain is always there, a constant reminder of what I lack. And the smile, once a beacon of hope, has become a burden that I carry with me everywhere I go.

I wear a smile upon my face,
A mask to hide the inner place.
It's there to shield the pain and strife,
And keep me going through this life.
But behind this facade, I hide,
A thousand sorrows deep inside.
For though I try to keep them locked away,
They always seem to find a way.
The fake smile that I wear so well,
Is just a cover for the hell.

And though I wish I could break free,
I fear what others might see.

The smile is a mask that I wear, a thin veil that covers the emptiness inside. It's a constant battle to keep up the charade, to pretend that everything is okay when it's not. But the smile is fading, and I fear that one day, it will disappear completely. Every day, I wake up and put on my smile, hoping that it will be enough to get me through the day. But as the hours pass, the smile fades, and I am left alone with my pain. It's a constant struggle to keep up appearances, to pretend that everything is okay when it's not.

The worst part is that no one sees the pain behind the smile. They see only what I want them to see, a happy and contented person with no troubles in the world. But the reality is very different. The pain is always there, a constant reminder of what I lack. And the smile, once a beacon of hope, has become a burden that I carry with me everywhere I go.

I wear a smile upon my face,
A mask to hide the inner place.
It's there to shield the pain and strife,
And keep me going through this life.
But behind this facade, I hide,
A thousand sorrows deep inside.
For though I try to keep them locked away,
They always seem to find a way.

The fake smile that I wear so well,
Is just a cover for the hell.
And though I wish I could break free,
I fear what others might see.

The smile is a mask that I wear, a thin veil that covers the emptiness inside. It's a constant battle to keep up the charade, to pretend that everything is okay when it's not. But the smile is fading, and I fear that one day, it will disappear completely. Every day, I wake up and put on my smile, hoping that it will be enough to get me through the day. But as the hours pass, the smile fades, and I am left alone with my pain. It's a constant struggle to keep up appearances, to pretend that everything is okay when it's not.

The worst part is that no one sees the pain behind the smile. They see only what I want them to see, a happy and contented person with no troubles in the world. But the reality is very different. The pain is always there, a constant reminder of what I lack. And the smile, once a beacon of hope, has become a burden that I carry with me everywhere I go.

14. The Empathic Pain

Empathic pain weighs heavy on my soul,
A burden that I cannot control.
It seeps into my very being,
And leaves me feeling lost and unseeing.
The pain of others becomes my own,
A weight that I cannot disown.
And though I try to ease their pain,
It seems like nothing will ever change.
The weight of empathic pain can crush,
And leave us feeling like we must
Surrender to the sadness and despair,
And let the weight take us to where.

Empathy is a blessing and a curse. On one hand, it allows me to feel the pain of others and connect with them on a deep level. But on the other hand, it's a weight that I carry with me wherever I go. The world's suffering is too much to bear, and I am left drowning in a sea of emotions.

The weight of empathic pain is a heavy burden to carry, and it's a struggle to find ways to cope with it. Sometimes, I find myself feeling overwhelmed by the pain of others, unable to separate their emotions from my own. It's like being trapped in a never-ending storm, with no way out.

The worst part is that I can't help but feel responsible for the pain of others. I know that it's not my fault, but I can't help but feel like I should be doing more to help. The weight of empathic pain is a constant reminder of my own limitations, of my own inability to fix the world's problems.

But despite the pain, I know that empathy is a gift. It allows me to connect with others on a deep level, to understand their pain and offer comfort. It's a reminder that we are all connected, that our pain and suffering is not unique to us alone. And even though the weight of empathic pain is heavy, I know that it's a burden worth bearing.

15. Hope In The Darkness

When all around is bleak and dim,
And shadows cloud your every whim,
When life seems like a cruel, cruel game,
And hope is but a fleeting flame.
Hold on, my dear, and do not fear,
For hope still lingers ever near,
In the darkest hour, it still shines bright,
A beacon of hope, a guiding light.
So hold on tight and don't let go,
Hope will help you weather the storm,
It will give you the strength to carry on,
And guide you safely through the unknown.
In the darkness, we may feel alone
Lost in the shadows, with no place to go
But in the midst of our despair
Hope is always there
It's the light that guides us through the night
The spark that ignites our inner fight
For hope is what sustains us
In the face of life's challenges
It's the strength to keep going
When everything else feels like it's slowing

The faith that things will get better
When we feel like we can't weather
So hold onto hope, my dear
Let it wipe away your tears
For even in the darkest of days
Hope will always find a way
It's the light that shines in the distance
The hand that helps us with our resistance
For hope is what sustains us
In the face of life's challenges
So let us hold onto hope
And find the strength to cope
For even in the darkest of times
Hope will always shine.

Life can be dark at times. We face challenges, loss, and uncertainty. It can be easy to lose hope during the darkness.

But hope is what sustains us. It's what keeps us moving forward, even when things seem impossible. It's the light that guides us through the darkness.

By holding onto hope, practicing self-compassion, and finding support from others, we can find the strength to keep going. We can learn to see the good amidst the bad, to hold onto faith in ourselves and the world, and to find joy in the journey. In the end, hope is what sustains us through the ups and downs of life.

16. Caught In The Crossfire Of Love

The miles may stretch, the distance wide,
But love can span the great divide,
Even though you may be far,
Your love still burns like a shining star.
The ache of separation may be hard to bear,
But love can keep you warm and fair,
It can bridge the gap and bring you near,
Even when distance fills you with fear.
So hold on to the love that binds,
For though you may be miles apart,
Your hearts beat as one, forever entwined,
A love that's pure, a work of art.

Love is a double-edged sword. It can be the source of immense joy and happiness, but it can also bring about heart-wrenching pain, especially when distance separates us from the ones we love. The feeling of longing, the emptiness in our hearts, the constant yearning for their touch - it's an excruciating experience that only those who have been through it can understand.

Being in a long-distance relationship is like living in a perpetual state of sadness. The physical distance creates a barrier that cannot be easily overcome, leaving us feeling isolated and alone. Virtual communication can only do so much to bridge the gap, but it can never truly replace the warmth of a real embrace or the comfort of being in each other's company.

The emotional strain of being in a long-distance relationship is immense. The constant fear of losing them, the nagging doubts about their faithfulness, and the overwhelming sense of loneliness can all take a toll on our mental health. It's a daily battle to keep the flame of love burning bright, even when it feels like it's about to flicker out.

But despite all the pain and struggles, we soldier on. We hold onto hope, cling to the love that we share, and pray that one day we'll be reunited with the one we love. In the end, love always finds a way.

17. Wounded Love

The world can be a cruel, cruel place,
With emotions that can leave a bitter taste,
Tragedy and loss, heartbreak and pain,
A world that sometimes feels insane.
But though the weight may be hard to bear,
And the news may seem too much to share,
There's always hope to be found,
A way to rise above the ground.
For even in the darkest hour,
There's light that shines with a gentle power,
A kindness, a love, a helping hand,
That can lift you up and help you stand.
So hold on tight and don't give in,
For hope will always be a win,
A light that shines, a beacon true,
That will guide you through and see you through.

Love can be a source of immense joy, but it can also be a source of heartbreak. The pain of a broken heart can be all-consuming, leaving us feeling shattered and alone.

The power of love can be healing. It can help us mend the wounds of heartbreak, find new hope, and move forward. It can remind us of the beauty of life and the importance of connection.

But healing from heartbreak is a journey. It requires a willingness to let go of the past, to forgive ourselves and others, and to open ourselves up to new possibilities.

By learning to let go of the past, practicing self-compassion, and opening ourselves up to new possibilities, we can begin to heal from the wounds of heartbreak. We can learn to love again, trust in the journey, and find joy in the midst of pain. For in the end, love always has the power to heal.

18. Society's Hollow Promise

Society's promises are empty and false,
A trap that leaves us feeling lost.
We chase after what we think we need,
And in the end, we're left to bleed.
We're told to fit a certain mold,
To do as we're told, to never be bold.
But in this conformity, we lose our souls,
And become just another face in the roles.
Society's promises are a lie,
A trap that we cannot deny.
But even as we struggle to be free,
We find ourselves bound by its decree.

Society is a hollow promise, a mirage that disappears as soon as we get close. It promises us happiness and fulfillment, but in reality, it's a trap that leaves us feeling empty and unfulfilled. It's a never-ending cycle of consumerism, where we are told that happiness can be found in material possessions.

But the reality is that society's promises are empty. No amount of money or possessions can fill the void inside us, and we are left feeling lost and alone. Society tells us that we need to conform to its ideals, to fit into its narrow mold. But in doing so, we lose sight of our own individuality and uniqueness.

The worst part is that society's messages are everywhere. We can't escape them, no matter how hard we try. They are in the advertisements we see, the movies we watch, and the books we read. They tell us that we need to be a certain way, that we need to look a certain way, and that we need to buy certain things in order to be happy.

But I know that this is a lie. Happiness cannot be found in material possessions or in conforming to society's expectations. It can only be found within ourselves, in our own unique passions and interests. And even though society's promises are hollow, I know that there is hope for something more.

Society's promises are empty and false,
A trap that leaves us feeling lost.
We chase after what we think we need,
And in the end, we're left to bleed.
We're told to fit a certain mold,
To do as we're told, to never be bold.
But in this conformity, we lose our souls,
And become just another face in the roles.
Society's promises are a lie,
A trap that we cannot deny.
But even as we struggle to be free,
We find ourselves bound by its decree.

Society is a hollow promise, a mirage that disappears as soon as we get close. It promises us happiness and fulfillment, but in reality, it's a trap that leaves us feeling empty and unfulfilled. It's a never-ending cycle of consumerism, where we are told that happiness can be found in material possessions.

But the reality is that society's promises are empty. No amount of money or possessions can fill the void inside us, and we are left feeling lost and alone. Society tells us that we need to conform to its ideals, to fit into its narrow mold. But in doing so, we lose sight of our own individuality and uniqueness.

The worst part is that society's messages are everywhere. We can't escape them, no matter how hard we try. They are in the advertisements we see, the movies we watch, and the books we read. They tell us that we need to be a certain way, that we need to look a certain way, and that we need to buy certain things in order to be happy.

But I know that this is a lie. Happiness cannot be found in material possessions or in conforming to society's expectations. It can only be found within ourselves, in our own unique passions and interests. And even though society's promises are hollow, I know that there is hope for something more.

Society's promises are empty and false,
A trap that leaves us feeling lost.

We chase after what we think we need,
And in the end, we're left to bleed.
We're told to fit a certain mold,
To do as we're told, to never be bold.
But in this conformity, we lose our souls,
And become just another face in the roles.
Society's promises are a lie,
A trap that we cannot deny.
But even as we struggle to be free,
We find ourselves bound by its decree.

Society is a hollow promise, a mirage that disappears as soon as we get close. It promises us happiness and fulfillment, but in reality, it's a trap that leaves us feeling empty and unfulfilled. It's a never-ending cycle of consumerism, where we are told that happiness can be found in material possessions.

But the reality is that society's promises are empty. No amount of money or possessions can fill the void inside us, and we are left feeling lost and alone. Society tells us that we need to conform to its ideals, to fit into its narrow mold. But in doing so, we lose sight of our own individuality and uniqueness.

The worst part is that society's messages are everywhere. We can't escape them, no matter how hard we try. They are in the advertisements we see, the movies we watch, and the books we read. They tell us that we need to be a certain way, that we need to look a certain way, and that we need to buy certain things in order to be happy.

But I know that this is a lie. Happiness cannot be found in material possessions or in conforming to society's expectations. It can only be found within ourselves, in our own unique passions and interests. And even though society's promises are hollow, I know that there is hope for something more.

Society's promises are empty and false,
A trap that leaves us feeling lost.
We chase after what we think we need,
And in the end, we're left to bleed.
We're told to fit a certain mold,
To do as we're told, to never be bold.
But in this conformity, we lose our souls,
And become just another face in the roles.
Society's promises are a lie,
A trap that we cannot deny.
But even as we struggle to be free,
We find ourselves bound by its decree.

Society is a hollow promise, a mirage that disappears as soon as we get close. It promises us happiness and fulfillment, but in reality, it's a trap that leaves us feeling empty and unfulfilled. It's a never-ending cycle of consumerism, where we are told that happiness can be found in material possessions.

But the reality is that society's promises are empty. No amount of money or possessions can fill the void inside us, and we are left feeling lost and alone. Society tells us that we need to conform to its ideals, to fit into its narrow mold. But in doing so, we lose sight of our own individuality and uniqueness.

The worst part is that society's messages are everywhere. We can't escape them, no matter how hard we try. They are in the advertisements we see, the movies we watch, and the books we read. They tell us that we need to be a certain way, that we need to look a certain way, and that we need to buy certain things in order to be happy.

But I know that this is a lie. Happiness cannot be found in material possessions or in conforming to society's expectations. It can only be found within ourselves, in our own unique passions and interests. And even though society's promises are hollow, I know that there is hope for something more.

Society's promises are empty and false,
A trap that leaves us feeling lost.
We chase after what we think we need,
And in the end, we're left to bleed.
We're told to fit a certain mold,
To do as we're told, to never be bold.
But in this conformity, we lose our souls,
And become just another face in the roles.
Society's promises are a lie,

A trap that we cannot deny.
But even as we struggle to be free,
We find ourselves bound by its decree.

Society is a hollow promise, a mirage that disappears as soon as we get close. It promises us happiness and fulfillment, but in reality, it's a trap that leaves us feeling empty and unfulfilled. It's a never-ending cycle of consumerism, where we are told that happiness can be found in material possessions.

But the reality is that society's promises are empty. No amount of money or possessions can fill the void inside us, and we are left feeling lost and alone. Society tells us that we need to conform to its ideals, to fit into its narrow mold. But in doing so, we lose sight of our own individuality and uniqueness.

The worst part is that society's messages are everywhere. We can't escape them, no matter how hard we try. They are in the advertisements we see, the movies we watch, and the books we read. They tell us that we need to be a certain way, that we need to look a certain way, and that we need to buy certain things in order to be happy.

But I know that this is a lie. Happiness cannot be found in material possessions or in conforming to society's expectations. It can only be found within ourselves, in our own unique passions and interests. And even though society's promises are hollow, I know that there is hope for something

more.
Society's promises are empty and false,
A trap that leaves us feeling lost.
We chase after what we think we need,
And in the end, we're left to bleed.
We're told to fit a certain mold,
To do as we're told, to never be bold.
But in this conformity, we lose our souls,
And become just another face in the roles.
Society's promises are a lie,
A trap that we cannot deny.
But even as we struggle to be free,
We find ourselves bound by its decree.

Society is a hollow promise, a mirage that disappears as soon as we get close. It promises us happiness and fulfillment, but in reality, it's a trap that leaves us feeling empty and unfulfilled. It's a never-ending cycle of consumerism, where we are told that happiness can be found in material possessions.

But the reality is that society's promises are empty. No amount of money or possessions can fill the void inside us, and we are left feeling lost and alone. Society tells us that we need to conform to its ideals, to fit into its narrow mold. But in doing so, we lose sight of our own individuality and uniqueness.

The worst part is that society's messages are everywhere. We can't escape them, no matter how hard we try. They are in the advertisements we see, the movies we watch, and the books we read. They tell us that we need to be a certain way, that we need to look a certain way, and that we need to buy certain things in order to be happy.

But I know that this is a lie. Happiness cannot be found in material possessions or in conforming to society's expectations. It can only be found within ourselves, in our own unique passions and interests. And even though society's promises are hollow, I know that there is hope for something more.

Society's promises are empty and false,
A trap that leaves us feeling lost.
We chase after what we think we need,
And in the end, we're left to bleed.
We're told to fit a certain mold,
To do as we're told, to never be bold.
But in this conformity, we lose our souls,
And become just another face in the roles.
Society's promises are a lie,
A trap that we cannot deny.
But even as we struggle to be free,
We find ourselves bound by its decree.

Society is a hollow promise, a mirage that disappears as soon as we get close. It promises us happiness and fulfillment, but in reality, it's a trap that leaves us feeling empty and unfulfilled. It's a never-ending cycle of consumerism, where we are told that happiness can be found in material possessions.

But the reality is that society's promises are empty. No amount of money or possessions can fill the void inside us, and we are left feeling lost and alone. Society tells us that we need to conform to its ideals, to fit into its narrow mold. But in doing so, we lose sight of our own individuality and uniqueness.

The worst part is that society's messages are everywhere. We can't escape them, no matter how hard we try. They are in the advertisements we see, the movies we watch, and the books we read. They tell us that we need to be a certain way, that we need to look a certain way, and that we need to buy certain things in order to be happy.

But I know that this is a lie. Happiness cannot be found in material possessions or in conforming to society's expectations. It can only be found within ourselves, in our own unique passions and interests. And even though society's promises are hollow, I know that there is hope for something more.

Society's promises are empty and false,
A trap that leaves us feeling lost.
We chase after what we think we need,
And in the end, we're left to bleed.

We're told to fit a certain mold,
To do as we're told, to never be bold.
But in this conformity, we lose our souls,
And become just another face in the roles.
Society's promises are a lie,
A trap that we cannot deny.
But even as we struggle to be free,
We find ourselves bound by its decree.

Society is a hollow promise, a mirage that disappears as soon as we get close. It promises us happiness and fulfillment, but in reality, it's a trap that leaves us feeling empty and unfulfilled. It's a never-ending cycle of consumerism, where we are told that happiness can be found in material possessions.

But the reality is that society's promises are empty. No amount of money or possessions can fill the void inside us, and we are left feeling lost and alone. Society tells us that we need to conform to its ideals, to fit into its narrow mold. But in doing so, we lose sight of our own individuality and uniqueness.

The worst part is that society's messages are everywhere. We can't escape them, no matter how hard we try. They are in the advertisements we see, the movies we watch, and the books we read. They tell us that we need to be a certain way, that we need to look a certain way, and that we need to buy certain things in order to be happy.

But I know that this is a lie. Happiness cannot be found in material possessions or in conforming to society's expectations. It can only be found within ourselves, in our own unique passions and interests. And even though society's promises are hollow, I know that there is hope for something more.

19. Love's Bittersweet Relief

Love is a balm for the wounded soul,
A relief that makes us whole.
It heals the wounds that life can bring,
And makes our hearts once again sing.
In the embrace of love, we find peace,
And all the pain and hurt release.
For though the world may be cruel and cold,
Love's warmth is something that cannot be sold.
So let us seek out love's sweet embrace,
And feel its power fill the space.
For in the end, it's love that we need,
To heal the wounds and help us succeed.

Love is a bittersweet relief, a salve for the wounds that we carry inside us. It's a reminder that we are not alone, that there is someone out there who understands us and accepts us for who we are. But it's also a reminder of our own vulnerabilities, of the pain that comes with opening ourselves up to another person.

Love is a double-edged sword, a constant battle between vulnerability and strength. It's a reminder that we are human, that we are capable of feeling both joy and pain. And even though it's bittersweet, I know that it's worth the risk.

The worst part is that love can be fleeting. It's not a guarantee, and there is always the risk of heartbreak. But even though the pain of losing love can be overwhelming, the relief that comes with finding it is worth the risk.

20. Courage To Love

The courage to love can be a daunting thing,
A journey that requires us to spread our wings.
To take a leap of faith and trust in another,
To let go of fear and embrace each other.
It takes strength to love in a world so cold,
To find a flame in a heart that's grown old.
But if we can find the courage to try,
We'll find a love that will never die.
For in the end, it's love that gives us hope,
And helps us to find the strength to cope.
So let us be brave and take a chance,
And let love lead us in this dance.

Courage for love is a necessary ingredient for a fulfilling life. It's the courage to open ourselves up to another person, to be vulnerable and honest about our emotions. It's the courage to take a chance on love, even though there is always the risk of heartbreak.

But the reality is that courage for love can be hard to come by. We may be afraid of rejection or afraid of being hurt. We may have been hurt in the past and fear that it will happen again.

The worst part is that without courage for love, we may miss out on something truly beautiful. We may miss out on the joy and fulfillment that comes with opening ourselves up to another person. But even though it's scary and uncertain, I know that having courage for love is worth the risk.

Epilogue: The Journey Continues

The journey of life is never done,
It twists and turns, it's never one,
But through it all, you've found a way,
To make it through each and every day.
With hope and courage, love and light,
You've found a way to make things right,
To overcome the darkness and the pain,
And find a path that's bright again.
So keep on going, never give up,
For life is a journey, and you're tough,
You've faced the storms and come out strong,
And found a way to keep moving on.

As I reflect on my life, I am left with only fragments of my experiences, shattered pieces of a once-beautiful world. And yet, even in this darkness, I hold on to the hope that one day, the fragments will come together once again, and the beauty of life will be restored.

In the end, perhaps the key to finding meaning and purpose in life is not to try to put the pieces together, but to embrace the fragments for what they are - small moments of beauty and joy that can sustain us through the trials and tribulations of life. It is only by accepting the fragility and impermanence of life that we can truly appreciate its beauty and find peace in the midst of sorrow.

Afterword

Life is full of challenges, uncertainties, and hardships. It can be easy to get caught up in the darkness and lose sight of the light. But it's important to remember that we are capable of resilience, growth, and transformation.

By embracing our struggles, practicing self-reflection, and finding support from others, we can navigate the ups and downs of life. We can find the beauty in the uncertainty, the hope in the darkness, and the courage to keep moving forward.

In the end, it's our resilience that defines us. We are capable of overcoming even the most difficult of obstacles, of finding joy in the midst of pain, and of holding onto hope for a better tomorrow. So let us embrace our struggles, hold onto hope, and find the strength to keep going.

Printed by Libri Plureos GmbH in Hamburg, Germany